# THEMATIC UN...

# Ice Cream

*Written by Dona Herweck Rice*

**Teacher Created Materials, Inc.**
P.O. Box 1040
Huntington Beach, CA 92647
©1997 Teacher Created Materials, Inc.
Made in U.S.A.

**ISBN-1-57609-117-3**

**Illustrated by**
*Barb Lorseyedi*

**Edited by**
*Karen J. Goldfluss, M.S. Ed.*

**Cover Art by**
*Chris Macabitas*

# Table of Contents

# Introduction

*Ice Cream* is a comprehensive thematic unit that uses the delicious, frozen treat as a basis for lessons across the curriculum. Its 80 pages are filled with a variety of activities, plans, and management tools that are sure to interest and motivate primary students while easing the teacher's workload. This literature-based thematic unit uses three high-quality selections at its core: *Curious George Goes to an Ice Cream Shop* by Margret Rey and Alan J. Shalleck, "Ice Cream" from Arnold Lobel's *Frog & Toad All Year*, and Ali Mitgutsch's classic nonfiction book, *From Milk to Ice Cream*. The students will experience language arts, math, science, social studies, art, music, physical education, and life skills through activities that connect each work of literature across the curriculum. In addition, many of the activities can be done cooperatively, enhancing everyone's learning experience.

This thematic unit includes the following:

❑ **Literature selections**—summaries of three children's books with related lessons (complete with reproducible pages) that cross the curriculum

❑ **Planning guides**—suggestions for introducing the unit, sequencing the lessons, and making projects and displays

❑ **Curriculum connections**—activities in language arts, math, science, social studies, art, music, physical education, and life skills that you can incorporate into your daily curriculum

❑ **Unit management suggestions**—teacher ideas for organizing this unit, including a bulletin board idea, incentives, patterns, and a unit award

❑ **Culminating activities**—class activities that will enrich the classroom experience and synthesize the learning

❑ **Bibliography**—suggested additional readings relating to the theme

---

To keep this valuable resource intact so it can be used year after year, you may wish to punch holes in the pages and store them in a three-ring binder.

---

# Introduction *(cont.)*

## Why a Balanced Approach?

The strength of a whole language approach is that it involves children in using all modes of communication: reading, writing, listening, speaking, illustrating, and doing. Communication skills are interconnected and integrated into lessons that emphasize the whole of language. Balancing this approach is our knowledge that every whole—including individual words—is composed of parts, and directed study of those parts can help a student to master the whole. Experience and research tell us that regular attention to phonics, other word-attack skills, spelling, and so forth, develop reading mastery, thereby fulfilling the unity of the whole-language experience. The child is thus led to read, write, spell, speak, and listen confidently in response to a literature experience introduced by the teacher. In these ways, language skills grow rapidly, stimulated by direct practice, involvement, and interest in the topic at hand.

## Why Thematic Planning?

One very useful tool for implementing a balanced language program is thematic planning. By choosing a theme with correlating literature selections for a unit of study, a teacher can plan activities throughout the day that lead to a cohesive, indepth study of the topic. Students will be practicing and applying their skills in meaningful contexts. Consequently, they will tend to learn and retain more. Both teachers and students will be freed from a day that is broken into unrelated segments of isolated drill and practice.

## Why Cooperative Learning?

Besides academic skills and content, students need to learn social skills. No longer can this area of development be taken for granted. Students must learn to work cooperatively in groups in order to function well in modern society. Group activities should be a regular part of school life, and teachers should consciously include social objectives as well as academic objectives in their planning. For example, a group working together to write a report may need to select a leader. The teacher should make clear to the students and monitor the qualities of good leader-follower group interactions, just as he/she would state and monitor the academic goals of the project.

## Why Big Books?

An excellent, cooperative, whole-language activity is the production of big books. Groups of students, or the whole class, can apply their language skills, content knowledge, and creativity to produce a big book that can become a part of the classroom library to be read and reread. These books make excellent culminating projects for sharing beyond the classroom with parents, librarians, other classes, and so forth. Big Books can be produced in many ways, and this thematic unit book includes directions for at least one method you may choose.

# Curious George Goes to an Ice Cream Shop

*by Margret Rey and Alan J. Shalleck*

## Summary

*He is at it again! The beloved, curious monkey finds himself in a brand-new ice cream shop in this tale that continues the tradition begun by favorite author H.A. Rey. This time, the man with the yellow hat leaves George in the ice cream shop while he leaves to run some errands. George, curious as always, begins to experiment with the ice cream scoop while the shop owner is busy taking a phone call. When the owner catches George, he shoos the monkey away, but soon George is back to his own brand of monkey business, building an enormous banana split while a crowd of onlookers watch from outside the shop's picture window. Once again, the shop owner catches George, but this time the crowd is cheering for the mischievous monkey. They begin to pour into the shop, bringing business and notoriety to the fledgling store. Just as always, all is well for George, and his curiosity saves the day.*

## Sample Plan

### Lesson 1

- Do one or more prereading activities (page 6).
- Make a class favorites graph (page 6).
- Explore at an ice cream center (page 6).
- Read aloud *Curious George Goes to an Ice Cream Shop.*
- Discuss the book (page 6).
- Send home a letter to the parents (page 77).

### Lesson 2

- Use sequencing strips (page 8) to sequence the story.
- Host an interview with Curious George (page 7).
- Relate favorite parts of the story (page 9).
- Complete a math activity (pages 10 and 11).
- Make a class big book (page 7).
- Do an ice cream freezing experiment (page 57).

### Lesson 3

- Complete a language arts activity (pages 10 and 11).
- Practice math skills (page 12).
- Make a class paper sundae (page 7).
- Read "Herbert Glerbett" and do the activity (page 32).
- Make a favorites graph for friends and family (page 40).

### Lesson 4

- Complete a social studies activity (pages 10 and 11).
- Create new ice cream flavors (page 31).
- Practice addition and money skills (page 46).
- Write about Ice Cream Facts (page 58).
- Make classroom chalkboard magnets (pages 72 and 74).

### Lesson 5

- Build an ice cream parlor (pages 7 and 69).
- Read "Eighteen Flavors" and do the activity (page 33).
- Color bookmarks (page 71) and have students create their own.
- Make Ice Cream in a Bag (page 67).

# Overview of Activities

## SETTING THE STAGE

1. Before you begin reading the book with your students, do some prereading activities to stimulate interest and enhance comprehension. Some activities you might try include the following:

   - Predict what the story might be about by reading the title and looking at the cover picture. Students are likely to be familiar with Curious George. Have the students relate other Curious George stories with which they are familiar.

   - Brainstorm how this story might be similar to other Curious George stories.

   - Answer some reading-interest questions: Do you like ice cream? Are you interested in stories about animals? What do you know about monkeys? Have you ever bought ice cream from an ice cream shop?

2. Prepare a center in the classroom with ice cream-related materials and a variety of ice cream books (see bibliography for suggestions). Send home a note (page 77) asking for necessary supplies. Ideas include different cones, scoops, jimmies, jars of sundae toppings, nuts, bowls, spoons, clean ice cream novelty wrappers, clean cartons, and more.

3. Create a class graph. To do so, reproduce the cone pattern on page 74 about six times. Reproduce the scoop pattern on page 73 as many times as you have students in your class (include yourself and any aides or parent volunteers present for this activity). On each of the cones, write a popular ice cream flavor. Vanilla, chocolate, and strawberry are three obvious choices. Neapolitan, rocky road, mint chocolate chip, and chocolate chip cookie dough are other popular flavors. On one cone be sure to write "other." Place these cones evenly along the bottom of a strip of butcher paper. Give each student a scoop of ice cream. Instruct the students to color their scoops according to their favorite flavors and to write their names on them. They can then affix their favorites in a stack on the appropriate cones. As a class, tally the scoops. (This can also be a lesson in tallying and counting by ones and fives.) Ask the students to name the favorite and least favorite flavors. As other teachers, students, and parents visit your room, add their favorites to your graph. Your graph can change throughout the unit, providing an ongoing lesson. Also see tallying activity on pages 40 and 41.

## ENJOYING THE BOOK

1. Read *Curious George Goes to an Ice Cream Shop* aloud to your class. Use variety and expression in your voice, engaging the students by your reading as well as the words. If desired, encourage the students to predict what might happen as you read aloud; however, it may prove more desirable to read the book through without interruption, allowing the students to experience the story as a whole and to engage their own thoughts about what they hear.

2. After the reading, discuss the book with the students. Ask if they have ever been to an ice cream shop like the one shown in the book. Also ask if they have ever been to a shop just after it was first opened. Allow them to share their stories and how they compare to George's experiences.

3. Share the book a second time, this time allowing the students to sequence the events while you read (page 8). Alternatively, they can sequence the story individually or as a class after the reading as an exercise in reading comprehension.

# Overview of Activities *(cont.)*

## ENJOYING THE BOOK *(cont.)*

4. Pretend that Curious George is visiting your classroom. Have the students answer the following questions according to how George might answer them:

   • What would it be like if you were to live with me in my house?
   • What would it be like if you came to our classroom as a student?
   • What would it be like if we played together as friends?

5. Have each student pick his or her favorite part of the book and illustrate it on page 9. Afterwards, have the students share their pictures and tell about their favorite parts. They can also make a graph, showing their favorites.

6. Have students solve the math problems on page 12 and then color the scoops according to the answers. The resulting picture will make a chocolate, vanilla, and strawberry sundae. If desired, change the problems for other skills.

7. Most ice cream names have many syllables. To extend the activity on page 31, provide a lesson on syllables and ask the students to create flavor names at least three syllables long.

## EXTENDING THE BOOK

1. The sundae-building activity on pages 10 and 11 can be used in two ways. Duplicate, color, and laminate the patterns for individual or small-group use or create a bulletin board. For the first method, have the students build a sundae by filling George's bowl with scoops of ice cream. For a math activity, write a total number in erasable ink on the bowl. Write addition or subtraction problems on the scoops, and instruct the students to fill the bowl with any problems the total of which is the number on the bowl. Also, the bowl's number can be a multiple of five, ten, or twenty, and each scoop can represent the base number. Students must fill the bowl by counting by fives, tens, etc. For language arts, write a word on the bowl and have the students fill it with synonyms, antonyms, homonyms, or other word combinations. Link scoops in the bowl to make compound words. For social studies, state/province names, direction words, or family names (aunt, father, etc.) can be placed in the bowl. The second method is to create a bulletin board, enlarge the patterns, color, and laminate for durability and reuse. Use one or more bowls, depending on your needs. Demonstrate any skill currently being studied in the same method as described above. The bulletin board can be interactive by allowing the students to build the sundae(s).

2. Make a class big book. On a large sheet of paper, allow each student to color a picture of him or herself and an ice cream treat of his or her own creation (like George's in the book). They can write a sentence about their creation, how it tastes, or how they feel when eating it. Bind the pages together in a class book with a student-drawn cover. Alternatively, allow the students to draw pictures of unusual ice cream treats, such as sardine sundaes or frozen carrots dipped in chocolate. Bind these pages together as before.

3. Make a class sundae either out of paper or (if parents can donate supplies) real ice cream. Allow each student to add a scoop. If using real ice cream, for health reasons be sure to divide the sundae into separate bowls before eating. A large paper sundae will make an entertaining wall decoration.

4. Build an ice cream parlor to use as a center area. Open a large appliance box to make two sides. These can serve as two walls against a corner of the classroom. Along one side of the box, cut a large picture window. On the inside, draw a counter and different ice creams. Place a table and chairs inside the parlor. (See page 69.)

# Sequencing the Story

**Directions:** Read the story. Cut apart the sentence strips. Put the strips in order and glue them to a blank piece of paper.

| |
|---|
| Mr. Herb answers a phone call. |
| The man with the yellow hat takes George to an ice cream shop. |
| Many people come into Mr. Herb's shop. |
| The shop owner says he has just opened the place. |
| George scoops ice cream into Mr. Herb's special order. |
| A crowd watches George. |
| Mr. Herb thanks George. |
| Mr. Herb is angry with George. |
| George builds a banana split at the front counter. |
| The man with the yellow hat chooses his flavor cone. |

# My Favorite Part

**Directions:** After reading *Curious George Goes to an Ice Cream Shop,* write about your favorite part.  Draw a picture to show what happens.

My favorite part of the book _____

_____

_____

_____

_____.

# Build a Sundae

For directions, see page 7, Extending the Book activity #1.

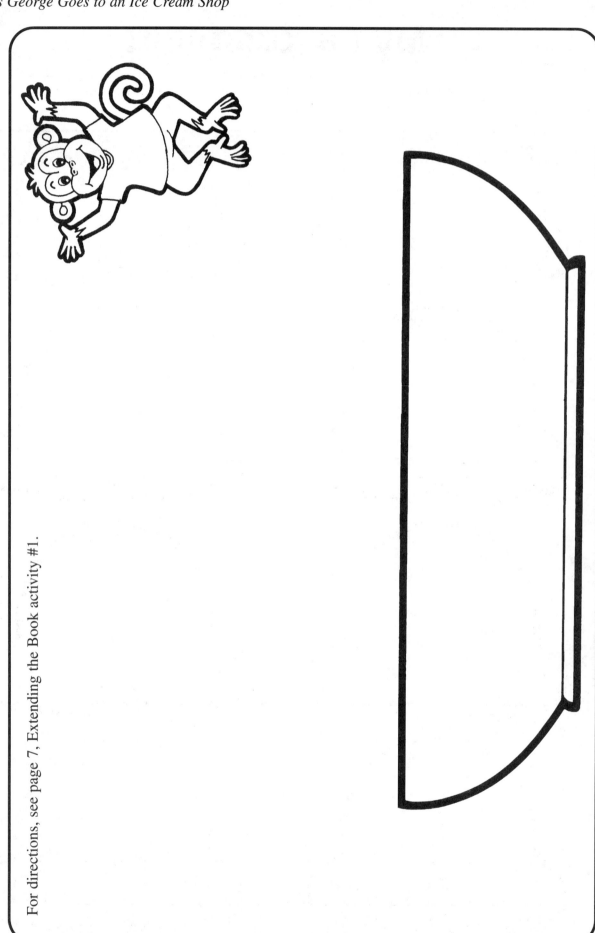

# Build a Sundae (cont.)

# Sundae Surprise

**Directions:** Solve the problems.  Color the scoops like this:

7 = brown  8 = white  9 = pink

# "Ice Cream"

## *by Arnold Lobel*

## Summary

*The story "Ice Cream" can be found in the book* Frog and Toad All Year. *In it, our heroes sit by a pond on a hot, summer day. Toad, being the good friend that he is, decides to go for some ice cream for Frog and himself. He arrives at the ice cream store without trouble and purchases two chocolate cones, but on his return trip the mishaps begin. The hot, summer sun easily melts the ice cream, and before he knows it, chocolate ice cream is dripping down Toad's head and over his body. He cannot see where he is walking, so he stumbles along the path while twigs and leaves stick to him as he goes. As Frog waits by the pond and wonders what is taking his friend so long, small animals race by him, running from a two-horned creature who is coming their way. When the creature arrives, Frog sees that it is Toad covered in ice cream with two cones sticking atop his head. Just then, Toad falls into the pond, and the ice cream is washed away. The story concludes with friendly cooperation as the two amphibians return together to the ice cream store, and there they eat their ice cream under the shade of a tree.*

## Sample Plan

### Lesson 1

- Complete one or more prereading activities (page 14).
- Share about adventures with a friend (page 14).
- Read and discuss "Ice Cream" (page 14).
- Make preparations for How the Ice Cream Cone Came to Be (pages 53–56).

### Lesson 2

- Host an interview with Toad (page 14).
- Use sequencing strips (page 16) to sequence the story.
- Learn about real frogs and toads (page 15).
- Make Clay Friends (page 17).
- Write nonsense rhymes (page 34).
- Work on the play (pages 53–56).

### Lesson 3

- Tell about My Favorite Part (page 18).
- Continue work on the play (pages 53–56).
- Learn about quarts and liters (pages 43 and 44).

- Begin writing an ice cream story (page 35).
- Make ice cream trucks (pages 63 and 64).

### Lesson 4

- Have students compare and contrast a friend with themselves (page 19).
- Observe melting (page 20).
- Complete writing an ice cream story (page 35).
- Fill in the missing math fact numbers (page 47).
- Continue work on the play (pages 53–56).

### Lesson 5

- Have an ice cream social (page 69).
- Present the play (pages 53–56).
- Make an Ice Cream Monster (page 21).
- Learn about taste buds (pages 59 and 60).

# Overview of Activities

## SETTING THE STAGE

1. Before you begin reading the book with your students, do some prereading activities to stimulate interest and enhance comprehension. Some activities you might try include the following:
   - Predict what the story might be about by reading the title and looking at the cover picture. Students are likely to be familiar with Frog and Toad. Ask them to relate other Frog and Toad adventures with which they are familiar.
   - Brainstorm how this story might be similar to other Frog and Toad stories.
   - Answer some reading-interest questions such as these: Do you have a best friend? If so, what sort of things do you do with one another? Are you interested in stories about amphibians? (Define *amphibian* for the class.) Have you ever eaten ice cream outside on a hot day? What happened?

2. Ask the students to write about or draw an adventure they have had with a good friend. They can write their stories on the ice cream stationery (page 75) or draw on plain paper. Allow the students to share their stories with the class. If desired, bind the stories in a class book titled "Friends" or another title of the students' choice.

## ENJOYING THE BOOK

1. Read "Ice Cream" aloud. Use variety and expression in your voice, engaging the students by your reading as well as the words. If desired, encourage the students to predict what might happen as you read aloud; however, it may prove more desirable to read the book through without interruption, allowing the students to experience the story as a whole and to engage their own thoughts about what they hear.

2. After the reading, discuss the book with the students. Ask if they have ever had a misadventure such as Toad experiences. Allow them to relate their stories and to compare them to the story in the book.

3. Share the book a second time, this time allowing the students to sequence the events while you read (page 16). Alternatively, they can sequence the story individually or as a class after the reading as an exercise in reading comprehension.

4. Make frogs and toads from clay. Follow the directions on page 17.

5. Pretend that Toad is visiting your classroom. Have the students answer the following questions according to how he might answer them:
   - What is your favorite thing about your friend, Frog?
   - Why did you go alone to get the ice cream?
   - How did it feel to have ice cream dripping and melting all over you?

6. Have each student pick his or her favorite part of the book and illustrate it, using page 18. Afterwards, have the students share their pictures and tell about their favorite parts. They can also make a graph, showing their favorites.

7. Page 19 is a contrast-comparison activity. Using the Venn diagram provided, ask each student to contrast and compare him/herself with a friend. Allow the students to choose any friend and to think of characteristics of themselves and their friends, putting mutual characteristics in the center place where the cones cross. Of course, instead of the term "characteristic" you may wish to use a simpler phrase such as "describing words that tell about you and a friend." It will be helpful to model this activity for the students before you begin, perhaps by completing a diagram about yourself and a good friend of yours.

# Overview of Activities *(cont.)*

## ENJOYING THE BOOK *(cont.)*

8. Choose either page 43 or 44 to work with standard or metric measurements, or you can complete both pages for a broader experience. When doing either, bring in an empty ice cream container in the quart or liter size so that students can have a hands-on experience. You might also bring in other measuring materials and items which the students can measure. Place these at a learning center for individual or small group use.

## EXTENDING THE BOOK

1. Distribute page 20 to each small group of students and have them work together. As a class, choose four different items that melt easily. Chocolate ice cream (as in the story) must be one of them. Other possible items are an ice cube, a frozen fruit bar, butter, a chocolate-covered ice cream bar, or a chocolate candy. Write the items on the chart. Place each of the four items directly from the freezer onto a large sheet of waxed paper and then place the items in the sun. Allow the students to watch what happens and to record their observations on the sheet provided. (If they are pre-writers, ask them to draw.) Afterwards, discuss the possible reasons why the items melted at different rates. Also discuss the likelihood of Toad being covered with melting ice cream by the time he reaches Frog.

2. Provide each student with a copy of page 21. Allow them to use the cone and ice cream shapes to create a monster (either of their own creation or that replicates Toad in the story). You might provide the patterns on colored paper or allow the students to make stencils of them, tracing them onto paper of their choice. After they have decided upon a creature, allow them to glue it to a piece of paper and to add details with markers or crayons.

3. Learn about frogs and toads. Provide reference materials that show the students the physical compositions of each as well as their behaviors, habitats, and life cycles. If possible, bring a live frog and toad into the classroom for the students to see. Then, discuss what the true events of a frog's or toad's day might be like as compared to the events related in the story. The students can complete a Venn diagram, showing the comparison. Use the diagram from page 19 or simply draw two intersecting circles on a paper or the board. This comparison would be a good whole-class or small-group project.

4. Have the students write animal ice cream stories of their own, using their imaginations to make the animals behave in ways unlike they would naturally, just as Arnold Lobel does in the Frog and Toad stories. Each student can choose a pair of animals (encourage variety) and then think about how those animals (with human characteristics) might behave around ice cream. Instruct them to write their stories and to provide at least one illustration. Bind each student's story into a book or bind all the stories together into a class book.

5. Create an incentive board for the students. Using the patterns on page 71, allow each student to color and decorate a cone, writing his or her name on it. Display the cones in a row in a convenient, open place in the room. Reproduce the scoop pattern many times in a variety of colors. Determine the purpose for your incentive board (for example, completed homework, attentive listening, or good classroom citizenship). When a student earns an incentive point, allow him or her to choose an ice cream "flavor" and to add it to his or her cone. If desired, a pre-determined number of cones can earn a prize such as a free homework night, extra recess, or a special pencil.

# Sequencing the Story

**Directions:** Read the story. Cut apart the sentence strips. Put the strips in order and glue them to a blank piece of paper.

| |
|---|
| A squirrel tells Frog that a creature is coming. |
| Toad falls in the pond. |
| Frog and Toad sit by the pond on a hot, summer day. |
| The hot sun begins to melt the cones. |
| Toad decides to get ice cream for Frog and himself. |
| Frog and Toad go together to buy chocolate cones. |
| Toad buys two chocolate cones. |
| Frog wants some ice cream. |
| A frightened mouse runs past Frog. |
| The cones drip all over Toad, covering him with ice cream. |

# Clay Friends

Students can create clay frog and toad friends using the materials and directions below.

**Materials:**

- modeling clay (store bought or homemade)
- waxed paper
- pointed ice cream cones
- toothpicks
- green and brown paint (nontoxic)
- paintbrushes
- cups and water for cleaning the paintbrushes

**Directions:**

1. Distribute a piece of modeling clay to each student, about the size of a tennis ball. (Directions for making a doughy clay can be found below.)
2. Divide the clay into thirds.
3. Take one of the thirds and roll it into a ball. This is the body of the frog or toad.
4. Take a second section (third) and divide it in half (which is one-sixth of the original size). Roll one half into a ball. This will be the head.
5. Pull two pinches off the remaining half of the clay used in the previous step. Roll each pinch into a ball. Place them atop the head to make the eyes.
6. Take all the remaining clay and roll it together. Divide it into fourths. These will be the legs and arms. Roll each piece into a tube and attach them to the body.
7. Using the tip of an ice cream cone, carefully press it into the back of the frog or toad. This will make the resting place for a cone when the sculpture is dry and painted.
8. Use a toothpick to draw on features such as a mouth, eye sockets, and webbing.
9. Let your clay dry or bake it as directed.
10. When dry, paint the sculpture, as desired. Use it as an ice cream cone holder. (Note: If you have a class party at the end of the unit, place each student's cone in his/her sculpture while waiting to fill the cones with ice cream.)

## Make Your Own Modeling Clay

**Materials:**

- ³/₄ cup (190 mL) salt
- 1 cup (250 mL) water
- 1 cup (250 mL) water
- bowl
- 3 cups (750 mL) flour
- spoon

**Directions:**

1. Mix the ingredients in the bowl with a spoon.
2. Make the dough pliable and smooth by molding it with your hands.
3. After making your sculpture, let it air dry for several days or bake it in a 250° F (130° C) oven for 2.5 hours or until completely dry.

# My Favorite Part

**Directions:** After reading "Ice Cream," write about your favorite part.  Draw a picture to show what happens.

My favorite part of the book is when _____

_____

_____

_____

# My Friend and Me

**Directions:** Think about yourself and a good friend of yours. In the area marked "Me," write words that describe only you. In the area marked "My Friend," write words that describe only your friend. In the area marked "Both," write words that describe both of you.

# Melting Observations

**Directions:** This is an observation chart. As you watch each item melting in the sun, write or draw what you see on the chart. Also, answer the questions.

| What does it look like . . . | Item 1 _____ | Item 2 _____ | Item 3 _____ | Item 4 _____ |
|---|---|---|---|---|
| . . . at the beginning? | | | | |
| . . . after 1 minute? | | | | |
| . . . after 3 minutes? | | | | |
| . . . when it is melted? | | | | |

Which item melted first? _____

Which item melted last? _____

# Ice Cream Monster

**Directions:** Use the cone and scoop shapes to make a monster like the one the animals think they see in "Ice Cream." Cut out the shapes and glue them to another paper. Add any details you want with crayons or markers.

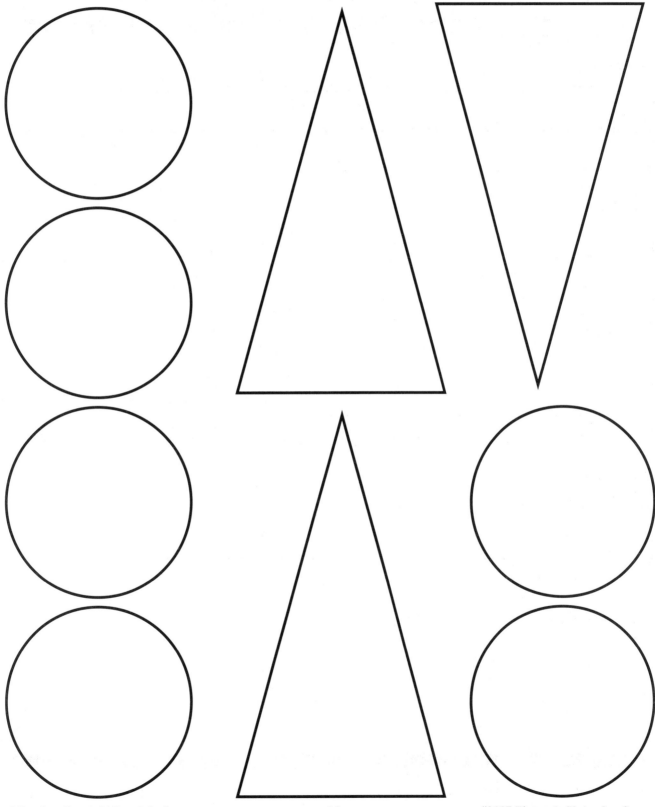

# From Milk to Ice Cream

## by Ali Mitgutsch

## Summary

*This nonfiction book tells the process of how ice cream is made. Clearly and simply written, the information is easily accessible to young readers, and the neat and colorful illustrations add to the book's charm and interest. Students will readily be able to understand the ice cream process from the comprehensive information provided.*

## Sample Plan

### Lesson 1

- Complete one or more prereading activities (page 23).
- Learn about pasteurization and homogenization (page 23).
- Read and discuss *From Milk to Ice Cream* (page 23).
- Learn more about how ice cream is made (pages 25 and 26).
- Interview an ice cream maker (page 23).

### Lesson 2

- Use the senses to complete the graph (page 24).
- Solve math problems to color the rainbow sundae (page 42).
- Sew ice cream cones (page 62).
- Imagine Ice Cream Personalities (page 36).
- Discover why the ice cream cone is ecologically sound (page 27).
- Create and advertise frozen treats (pages 28 and 29).

### Lesson 3

- Learn about ice cream ingredients (page 30).
- Play language arts games and puzzles (page 37).

- Review skills with the Clothespin Game (page 45).
- Practice estimating (page 50).
- Learn about the history of ice cream (pages 51 and 52).

### Lesson 4

- Unscramble ice cream words (page 38).
- Play the Build a Sundae Game (pages 48 and 49).
- Make ice cream collages (page 62).
- Run relays (page 66).
- Learn about antonyms (page 39).
- Bake ice cream (page 61).

### Lesson 5

- Review additional skills with the Clothespin Game (page 45).
- Build an ice cream truck (page 69).
- Sing ice cream songs (page 65).
- Make Coffee Can Ice Cream (page 68).
- Present unit awards (pages 76).

# Overview of Activities

## SETTING THE STAGE

1. Before you begin reading the book with your students, do some prereading activities to stimulate interest and enhance comprehension. Some activities you might try include:
   - Predict what the book might be about by reading the title and looking at the cover picture.
   - Brainstorm about ice cream and how it might be made. Ask the students to describe where and how the frozen treat is created. Write their ideas on the board or a sheet of butcher paper and keep them on display until after you have read the book.
   - Ask the students if any of them have been to a dairy or ice cream factory. If so, ask them to relate their experiences.
   - Brainstorm for ways in which you can find out about how ice cream is made. Students should list such things as looking in the library and visiting a factory. They are likely to have many more ideas, as well. Accept all their ideas and encourage their creative thinking.
   - Answer some reading-interest questions: Do you like ice cream? What is your favorite thing about it? Do you know how any food is made? Share what you know with the class How does ice cream stay frozen from the time it is made until you buy it at the store?
2. Ask students to write or draw about a cooking or food preparation experience they have had. They can write their stories on the ice cream stationery (page 75) or draw on plain paper. Allow the students to share their stories with the class. If desired, bind the stories in a class book entitled Our Cooking Experiences or another title of the students' choice.
3. Define *pasteurization* and *homogenization*. (*Pasteurization* is the process of sterilizing a liquid by heating it. *Homogenization* is the process of mixing thoroughly so all ingredients are well blended and smooth.) Tell the students what these processes do and why they are important in the production of many dairy foods.

## ENJOYING THE BOOK

1. Read *From Milk to Ice Cream* aloud. Use expression in your voice, engaging the students by your reading as well as the words. Nonfiction read aloud has a way of becoming humdrum unless the reader gives the sense that he or she enjoys the writing.
2. After the reading, discuss the book with the students. Have them compare the facts about how ice cream is made with their predictions. As a class, point out the accuracies of their guesses as well as the ways in which they differed from the reality of the process.
3. Share the book a second time. Afterwards, distribute page 25 to each student. Read the page together. Discuss any new or difficult words. Point out how the page provides the same information as the book in a slightly different way. Next, distribute page 26. Ask the students to cut apart the steps and to glue them onto another piece of paper in their correct order. They can use page 25 to help them. If there is time, also allow them to color the pictures according to their favorite ice cream flavors.
4. Pretend that an ice cream maker is visiting your classroom. Have the students answer the following questions according to how he or she might answer them:
   - What is your favorite thing about your job?
   - Why do you think there are so many different ice cream flavors?
   - How are the different flavors made?
   - Can you list some of the things you know of that have been added to plain vanilla ice cream to make different flavors?

# Overview of Activities *(cont.)*

## ENJOYING THE BOOK *(cont.)*

5. Page 27 provides an activity in ecology. Read it over with the students and have them answer/do one or more of the activities listed.

6. Have a class discussion about favorite frozen desserts. Let the students know that new frozen treats are frequently being invented, and now is their opportunity to be inventors. They are each to imagine a new frozen treat as well as its package. Then, on page 28, they can name their product, describe it and its package, and draw them both. On page 29, students can create a billboard advertisement for their new product. Each student should brainstorm for ideas first, keeping in mind that the idea is to convince others to buy the product. Color and catchy phrases do a lot for advertisements, as do humor and celebrity endorsements, among other things. Students can draw their billboards in the space on page 29 and then share them and their product ideas with the class.

7. Learn more about what goes inside manufactured ice cream by doing the activity on page 30. Begin by telling the students that for something to be called ice cream, it must meet certain government standards. For example, ice cream must have at least ten percent milk fat. Look at the labels on several kinds of ice cream, and you will be able to see the most common ingredients. Ingredients are listed in order from the most used to the least. Before looking at any labels, you might have the students predict what the biggest ingredient is. (Milk and cream are the best answers.) To do the activity on page 30, choose a method that is best for your class. Very young children can simply choose any of the ingredients that go into ice cream, making sure that one is a milk product. Older students can study various ice cream cartons. Then they can create labels that include the ingredients found in one kind of ice cream.

8. When preparing the activity on page 38, fold over the bottom before duplicating if you do not want the words to appear on the page.

9. The clothespin game on page 45 can be used to teach or reinforce addition and subtraction facts, shapes and shape words, greater and less than, or fraction parts. This page can also be used for language arts concepts such as blends and word endings, homonyms, synonyms, definitions, and more.

10. Set up a learning center to practice estimation. You will need one ice cream scoop, copies of page 50, and a variety of small items to scoop such as beans, beads, pebbles, popcorn kernels, candies, and nuts. Students should first estimate the number of items they think it will take to fill the scoop. Students work with partners to then practice scooping, counting, and correcting their estimates.

## EXTENDING THE BOOK

1. Take a class field trip to a dairy or ice cream factory. Bring along copies of page 25 or the book *From Milk to Ice Cream* in order to compare your learning with what is actually done at the factory you visit.

2. Provide one small scoop of ice cream and a spoon to each student. (For students with allergies and/or lactose intolerance, provide substitute ice cream products.) Ask the students to write about their sensory experiences: What the flavor looks, feels, sounds, and smells like.

3. Make a class cookbook. Begin with the recipes in this book (pages 57, 61, and 67 and 68) and add others of your own. Students can also bring in recipes from home. They can be for making ice cream or for making something that uses ice cream as an ingredient.

# How Ice Cream Is Made

**Directions:** Here is a model of how the ingredients for ice cream move through the factory to become the ice cream you buy at the store. Read it so you know the steps. Once you have learned the steps, solve the problem on page 26.

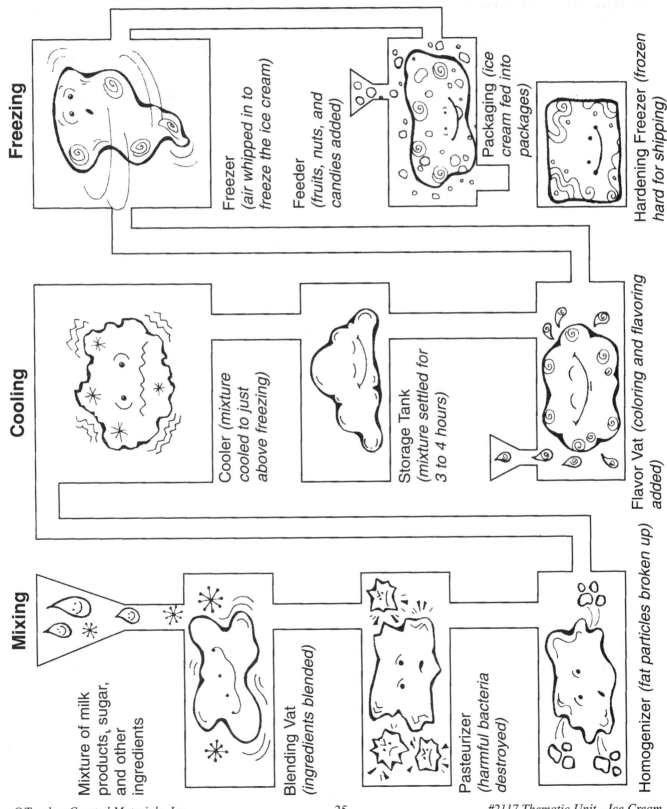

**Freezing**

Freezer *(air whipped in to freeze the ice cream)*

Feeder *(fruits, nuts, and candies added)*

Packaging *(ice cream fed into packages)*

Hardening Freezer *(frozen hard for shipping)*

**Cooling**

Cooler *(mixture cooled to just above freezing)*

Storage Tank *(mixture settled for 3 to 4 hours)*

Flavor Vat *(coloring and flavoring added)*

**Mixing**

Mixture of milk products, sugar, and other ingredients

Blending Vat *(ingredients blended)*

Pasteurizer *(harmful bacteria destroyed)*

Homogenizer *(fat particles broken up)*

# How Ice Cream Is Made *(cont.)*

**Directions:** All of his co-workers are sick, and Jamaal must make Moo Cow Ice Cream by himself. He is worried because he is not sure he remembers the steps in order. Can you help him? Arrange these cards in order and glue them on a chart that he can hang at his workstation.

| | |
|---|---|
| **Freeze Until Hard** | **Mix and Blend** |
| **Package** | **Pasteurize** |
| **Whip and Freeze** | **Add Coloring and Flavoring** |
| **Add Fruits, Nuts, and Candies** | **Store** |
| **Cool** | **Homogenize** |

# The Only Ecologically Sound Package

**Directions:** Someone once said, "The ice cream cone is the only ecologically sound package known." Think about this statement. What do you think it means? Discuss it, as well as the need for other ecologically sound packaging. Then do one or more of the following:

1. Create (or find) packages for other foods that are good for the environment. For example, why not use a pretzel as a lollipop stick? Write your ideas below.
2. What unnecessary packaging can you discover? List at least five examples below.
3. What reasons do you think companies have for unnecessary packaging? Give and explain at least one reason. Write or draw your answer below.

# Designing a New Ice Cream

**Directions:** Try your hand at designing a new ice cream and its package. Name and draw both here. Then do the activity on the next page.

Name of Product: _____

Description of Product: _____

Description of Package: _____

Product

Package

# Advertising Your Ice Cream

**Directions:** Now that you have designed a new product and package, you want the world to know about it. In the space below, design a billboard advertisement that will make people want to buy your new ice cream.

# Ice Cream: What's Inside?

**Directions:** What goes into ice cream?  Look at a real ice cream carton and then look at the ingredients listed below.  Choose the matching ingredients.  Cut them out and glue them onto the label of the ice cream carton.  If some ingredients are not given, add them in the empty boxes.  Do not forget to name your ice cream.

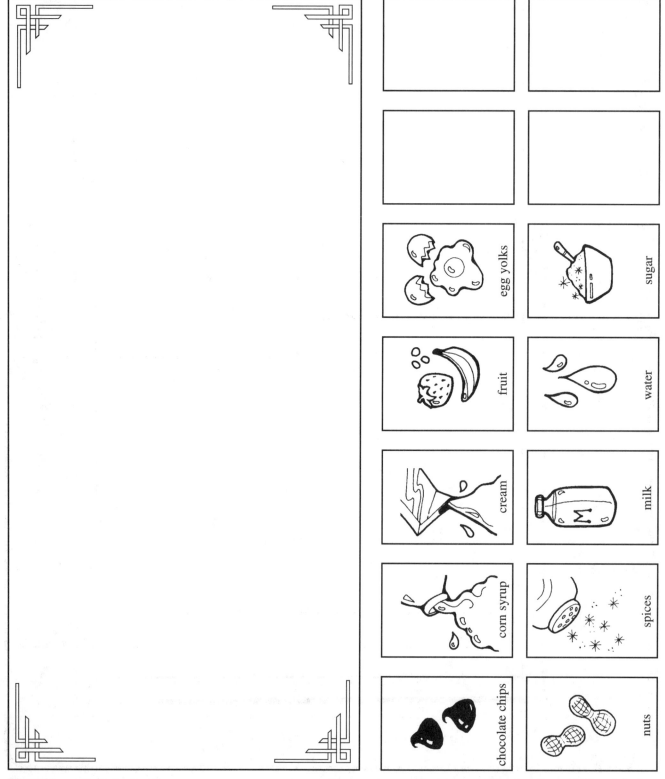

# Superduperiffic Ice Cream

**Directions:** Read (or listen to) "Bleezer's Ice Cream" by Jack Prelutsky from *The New Kid on the Block*. Pretend you are in charge of creating new flavors for Bleezer's freezer.

Write the names of six new creations here.

_____

_____

_____

_____

_____

_____

Your flavors are so popular that other stores want your recipes. Write one recipe here.

_____

**Ingredients:**

_____      _____

_____      _____

_____      _____

_____      _____

**Procedure:**

_____

_____

_____

_____

# You Are What You Eat

**Directions:** Read (or listen to) "Herbert Glerbett" by Jack Prelutsky in *The Random House Book of Poetry for Children*. Herbert is a boy who eats "sherbet by the pound" and eventually becomes a big, gooey, glob of green sherbet. Imagine you are Herbert and have become a glob of sherbet. Use your imagination to write your thoughts and feelings here.

# Umpteen Flavors

**Directions:** Read (or listen to) "Eighteen Flavors" by Shel Silverstein in *Where the Sidewalk Ends*. In the poem, Silverstein mentions 18 different flavors of ice cream. On the lines below, write all the real flavors you can think of. How many can you name?

My Flavor Collection

# I Scream, You Scream

**Directions:** There is a popular poem about ice cream that goes like this:

I scream,
You scream,
We all scream
For ice cream!

Write and illustrate your own version of the poem by changing the word "scream" to another word and then changing the last line with something else that rhymes.  Here are two examples:

I wish,
You wish,
We all wish
For jellyfish!

I squeal,
You squeal,
We all squeal
For banana peels!

Write your poem here:

_____

_____

_____

_____

_____

_____

_____

# Ice Cream Writing

**Directions:** Choose one of the titles below. Write your own ice cream story that tells what happens. (Use the ice cream stationery on page 75.)

## Story Titles

Life on Ice Cream Mountain

If Ice Cream Were the Only Food

Locked in the Ice Cream Store Overnight

The Day the Ice Cream Freezer Failed

The Day It Snowed Ice Cream

How Hot Fudge Was Invented

Before There Was Ice Cream

The First Ice Cream

Before There Were Ice Cream Cones

The Luscious Ice Cream Factory

The North Pole Is Really Made of Ice Cream

The Ice Cream Fairy

The King of Ice Cream Land

The Last Ice Cream Cone in the World

Pickle Ice Cream

The Boy Who Hated Ice Cream

The Girl Who Loved Ice Cream

The Ice Cream Goblin

The Ice Cream Parade

The Mouse in the Ice Cream Store

The Dog Who Loved Ice Cream

The Classroom Ice Cream Party

*Language Arts*

# Ice Cream Personalities

**Directions:** Imagine that each of the flavors below was a person. What would those people be like? Use your imaginations. You can make them anything you want them to be. For example, Vanilla Fudge might be a little boy who often gets into mischief or she might be a girl who loves to dance ballet. Write about or draw a person named for each flavor.

| Strawberry Swirl | Banana Fudge |
|---|---|
| | |
| **Chocolate Ripple** | **Cookies and Cream** |
| | |

# Ice Cream Games and Puzzles

**Directions:** Complete each of the games or puzzles.

1. Write all the words you can think of that have to do with ice cream.  The list has been started for you.

scoop _____   _____   _____   _____

cold _____   _____   _____   _____

freeze _____   _____   _____   _____

_____   _____   _____   _____

2. Spell all the words you can with the letters in STRAWBERRY ICE CREAM CONE.  The list has been started for you.

cob _____   _____   _____   _____

rot _____   _____   _____   _____

sew _____   _____   _____   _____

_____   _____   _____   _____

3. Fill in the crossword puzzle with the words in the cone.

mint
vanilla
chocolate
sundae
ice cream
frozen

# Ice Cream Scramble

**Directions:** Unscramble the letters to spell the ice cream flavors listed at the bottom of the page.

1. tnmi _____

2. alvanli _____

3. pnaeotlnai _____

4. mcaarle lwsri _____

5. liavlna egfud _____

6. teccohlao _____

7. hmoac _____

8. hltccooea phic _____

9. rsrtrwbeya _____

10. lmbbuugbe _____

11. enmlo _____

12. ykcro ador _____

13. miel _____

14. tebtur apcne _____

15. geduf pelpri _____

## Ice Cream Flavors

| | | |
|---|---|---|
| bubblegum | fudge ripple | Neapolitan |
| butter pecan | lemon | rocky road |
| caramel swirl | lime | strawberry |
| chocolate | mint | vanilla |
| chocolate chip | mocha | vanilla fudge |

# Ice Cream Antonym Poems

**Teacher Directions:**

1. As a class, brainstorm for adjectives to describe ice cream. Write these words on the board or overhead projector. Tell the students the words are called adjectives.

2. Again as a class, write the opposite of each word. Tell the students that these opposites are called antonyms.

3. Instruct students (or student pairs) to put each adjective-antonym pair into the poem frame below. Students will also need to fill in two other treats as directed. (Before students begin their poems, you may wish to provide the sample poem on the right.)

*Ice cream is sweet,*

*Sugar is, too.*

*Lemonheads™ are sour,*

*But yummy for you!*

---

Ice cream is _____,
(adjective)

_____ is (are), too.
(another treat)

_____ is (are)
(another treat)

_____,
(adjective)

But yummy for you!

---

# Favorite Flavors

**Directions:** Ask your family and friends what their favorite flavors are.  Be sure to ask at least ten people.  Do not forget to ask yourself!  Write each person's name and favorite flavor in the chart below.  Use the back if you need more room.  Then turn to page 41.

|  Name |  Favorite Flavor |
|------|-----------------|
|      |                 |
|      |                 |
|      |                 |
|      |                 |
|      |                 |
|      |                 |
|      |                 |
|      |                 |
|      |                 |

# Favorite Flavors *(cont.)*

**Directions:** Fill in the tally sheet on this page with the information from the last page. (Write one flavor in each box below.) You will need to write in each of the ice cream choices from your favorites chart. Under each choice, mark a tally ( I ) each time the favorite is chosen. Remember that each time you reach five in the tally, you mark it like this ( ⊦⊦⊦⊤ ).

Add up your tally totals on the tally sheet and then answer the questions at the bottom of the page.

| Favorite Flavors | Tally Marks | Totals |
|---|---|---|
|  |  |  |
|  |  |  |
|  |  |  |
|  |  |  |
|  |  |  |
|  |  |  |
|  |  |  |
|  |  |  |
|  |  |  |
|  |  |  |

Which flavor is the most popular? _____

Which flavor is the least popular? _____

# Rainbow Sundae

**Directions:** Solve the problems.  Color the sundae like this:

10 = yellow       12 = red       14 = orange       16 = pink
11 = purple       13 = blue       15 = green       17 = brown

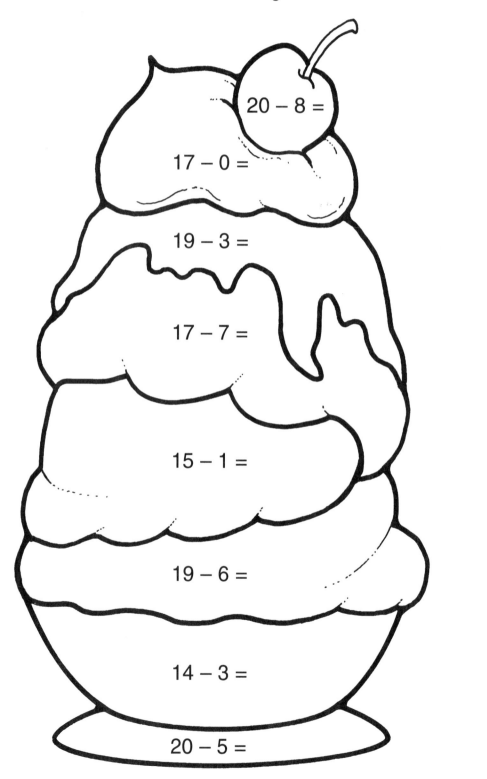

20 – 8 =

17 – 0 =

19 – 3 =

17 – 7 =

15 – 1 =

19 – 6 =

14 – 3 =

20 – 5 =

*Math*

# Measuring Ice Cream Quarts

**Directions:** Did you know that each person eats an average of 15 quarts of ice cream each year? That is a lot of ice cream! In order to better understand the size of a quart, cut out the measuring patterns. Trace them to make as many copies as directed. Use the patterns to answer the questions.

1. How many quarts are in a gallon?_____

2. How many pints are in a quart?_____

3. How many cups are in a pint?_____

4. How many cups are in a quart?_____

5. How many cups are in a gallon?_____

6. How many pints are in a gallon?_____

cup
(Make 16.)

gallon
(Make 1.)

pint
(Make 8.)

quart
(Make 4.)

©*Teacher Created Materials, Inc.*     43     *#2117 Thematic Unit—Ice Cream*

# Measuring Ice Cream Liters

**Directions:** Did you know that each person eats an average of 14 liters of ice cream each year? That is a lot of ice cream! In order to better understand the size of a liter, cut out the measuring patterns. Trace them to make as many copies as directed. Use them to answer the questions.

1. How many centiliters are in a deciliter?_____

2. How many deciliters are in a liter?_____

3. How many liters are in a decaliter?_____

   You can ask your parents for help with the next two.

4. Challenge: How many deciliters are in a decaliter?_____

5. Challenge: How many centiliters are in a decaliter?_____

decaliter
(Make 1.)

10 centiliters
(Make 1.)

deciliters
(Make 10.)

liter
(Make 10.)

# Clothespin Game

**Teacher Directions:** Reproduce the game board wheel. Color it and write in any math skill you wish to reinforce. Cut out the wheel and laminate it. Mark clothespins with the answers. Allow students to match the answers to the problems by affixing the clothespins.

To make the game board generic, label it with a dry-erase marker after it has been laminated. Then simply wipe it clean and relabel when you want to go to a different concept. You can also use a permanent marker and erase it with hairspray or nail polish remover.

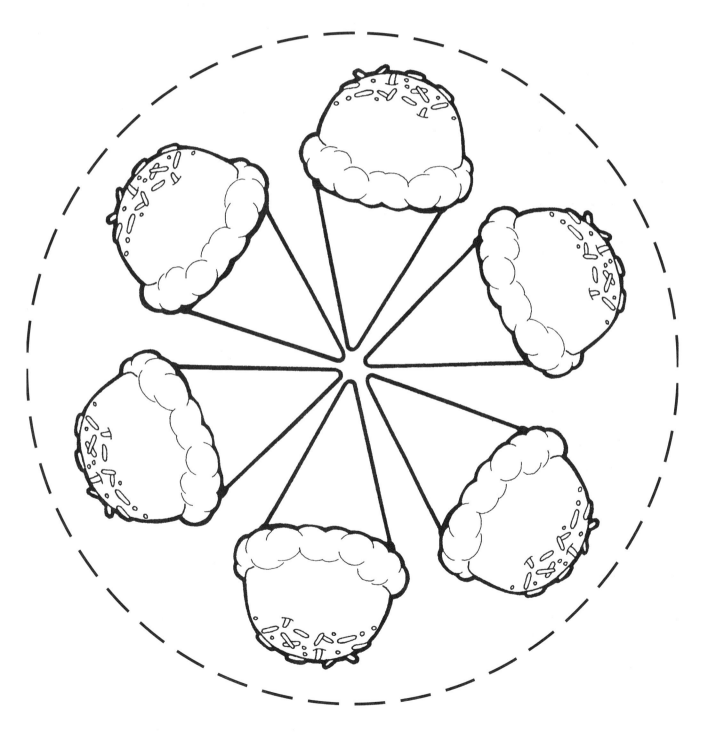

*Math*

# A Visit to the Ice Cream Store

**Directions:** Use the menu to solve the problems.

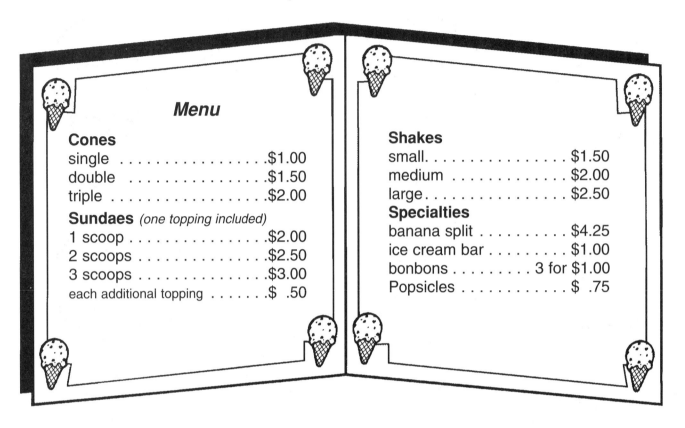

### Menu

**Cones**
single . . . . . . . . . . . . . . .$1.00
double . . . . . . . . . . . . .$1.50
triple . . . . . . . . . . . . . . .$2.00

**Sundaes** *(one topping included)*
1 scoop . . . . . . . . . . . . . .$2.00
2 scoops . . . . . . . . . . . . .$2.50
3 scoops . . . . . . . . . . . . .$3.00
each additional topping . . . . . .$ .50

**Shakes**
small. . . . . . . . . . . . . . $1.50
medium . . . . . . . . . . . $2.00
large. . . . . . . . . . . . . $2.50
**Specialties**
banana split . . . . . . . . . $4.25
ice cream bar . . . . . . . . $1.00
bonbons . . . . . . . . 3 for $1.00
Popsicles . . . . . . . . . . . $ .75

1. The Sweet family orders 1 double scoop cone, one 2-scoop sundae with 1 extra topping, 1 large shake, and 1 order of bonbons. What is the total bill?

2. Frances Freeze wants a 3 scoop sundae with 2 extra toppings and a popsicle. What will it cost her?

3. Carl Cold can eat 1 triple-scoop cone, 1 medium shake, 1 ice cream bar, and a popsicle for his dessert. If he buys all of that, what will his total bill be?

4. Homer Hot Fudge loves sundaes. He ordered a 3-scoop sundae with 5 extra toppings and 1 large shake to wash it down. He bought his daughter, Sherry Cherry, a banana split. What did all this food cost him?

# What's the Scoop?

**Directions:** Fill in the missing number on each cone to complete the problem.

1.

```
  10
+
  16
```

2.

```
  17
-
   8
```

3.

```
   4
+
  17
```

4.

```
   9
+
  19
```

5.

```
   8
-
   1
```

6.

```
  15
+
   4
```

7.

```
  11
-
   7
```

8.

```
  21
-
  16
```

9.

```
  20
+
  29
```

10.

```
  14
-
   7
```

11.

```
  13
-
  10
```

12.

```
  14
+
  25
```

13.

```
  14
-
   6
```

14.

```
  13
+
  19
```

15.

```
  12
+
  12
```

16.

```
  18
-
   6
```

# Build a Sundae Game

**Teacher Directions:**

1. Duplicate the game rules and laminate them for durability. Affix them to the front of a large envelope or file folder.

2. Duplicate, color, laminate, and cut out multiple copies of the patterns on the next page. Store them in the envelope or folder.

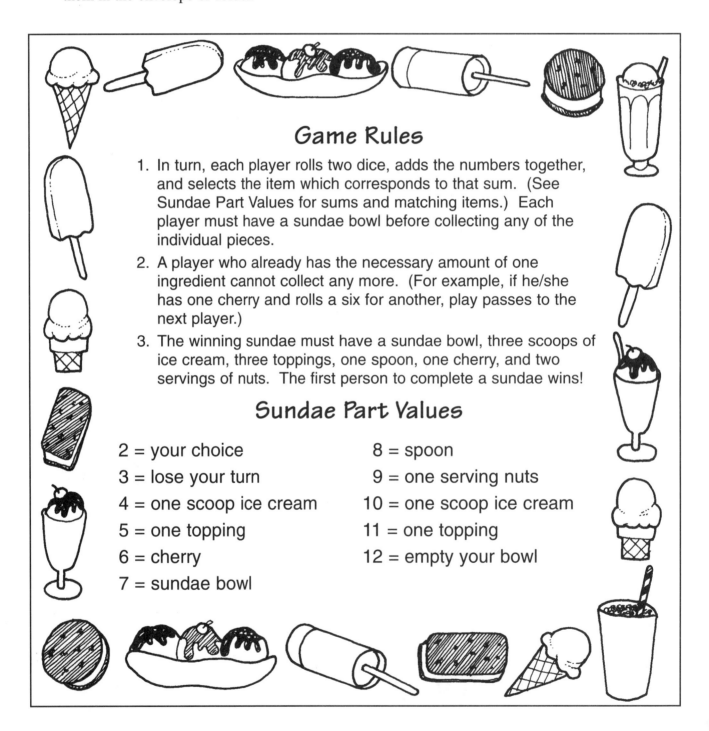

## Game Rules

1. In turn, each player rolls two dice, adds the numbers together, and selects the item which corresponds to that sum. (See Sundae Part Values for sums and matching items.) Each player must have a sundae bowl before collecting any of the individual pieces.

2. A player who already has the necessary amount of one ingredient cannot collect any more. (For example, if he/she has one cherry and rolls a six for another, play passes to the next player.)

3. The winning sundae must have a sundae bowl, three scoops of ice cream, three toppings, one spoon, one cherry, and two servings of nuts. The first person to complete a sundae wins!

## Sundae Part Values

2 = your choice

3 = lose your turn

4 = one scoop ice cream

5 = one topping

6 = cherry

7 = sundae bowl

8 = spoon

9 = one serving nuts

10 = one scoop ice cream

11 = one topping

12 = empty your bowl

# Build a Sundae Game *(cont.)*

**patterns**

# Estimating

**Directions:**

1. Choose one item and estimate (guess) how many it will take to fill one ice cream scoop.
2. Fill the scoop level with the item.
3. Count and write down the actual number in the scoop.
4. Figure out the difference between your estimate and the actual number.  Write down the difference.
5. Do these steps again for another item.

| Item | Estimate | Actual | Difference |
|------|----------|--------|------------|
|      |          |        |            |
|      |          |        |            |
|      |          |        |            |
|      |          |        |            |
|      |          |        |            |
|      |          |        |            |
|      |          |        |            |

# Where Is It?

**Directions:** Read the ice cream history facts. Then find each of the fact places on the map on page 52. Write each fact's number in the correct place on your map.

 **Rome:** Two thousand years ago, the Roman Emperor Nero liked to eat a treat made of ice, fruit, and honey. This marks the beginning of ice cream.

 **China:** In 1295 Marco Polo brought ice milk from China to Italy. He used milk from a yak and added sugar to make it sweet.

 **France:** In 1533 an Italian married King Henry of France and brought ice cream with her. A Frenchman opened an ice cream shop and became the first to add flavors like chocolate and strawberry.

 **England:** After 1533 ice cream traveled from France to England. English colonists brought their recipes to the New World in America.

 **Washington, D.C.:** Two hundred years ago, George Washington ate America's first ice cream in the place that is now called Washington, D.C.

 **Maryland:** In 1851 Jacob Fussell sold ice cream from a truck. He was also the first to make ice cream in a factory.

 **New York:** In 1903 Italo Marchiony received the first patent for an ice cream cone.

# Where Is It? *(cont.)*

Use the map below to find the places mentioned on page 51. Write the correct numbers in the boxes.

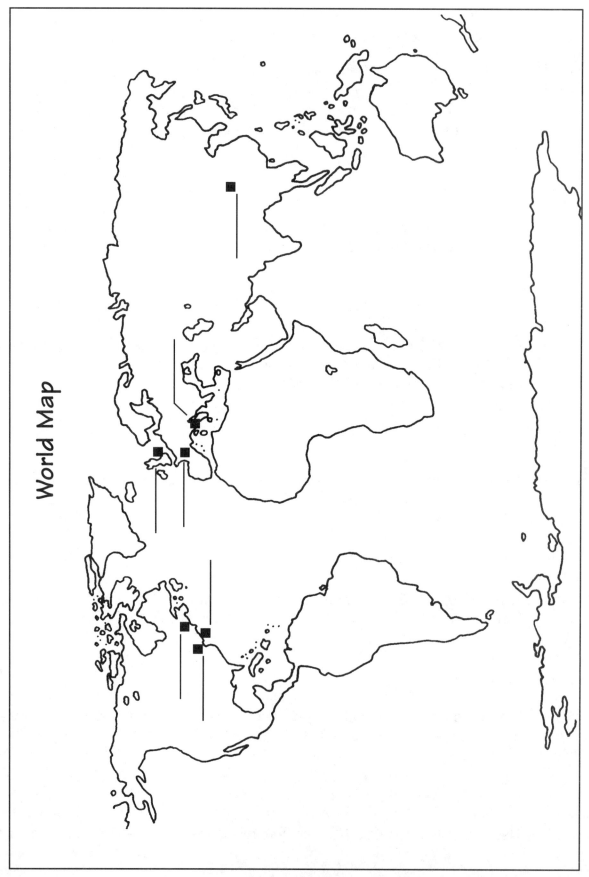

World Map

52

# How the Ice Cream Cone Came to Be

## Play Preparation

The history of the ice cream cone is an interesting one. On the following two pages is a short play that reenacts the actual event. (Although the play itself is fiction, it is based in fact.) At the bottom of this page is an encapsulated history. Read the history information to the class, or use it as a general reference. Then either read the play, assigning parts to willing students, or prepare sets and costumes and enact the play for parents, other classes, or whomever you choose. The performance might be an enjoyable part of a culminating party for the unit, during which ice cream is served and the unit's projects are displayed for parents to see.

In order to prepare for the play, you will need two large appliance boxes. Cut and decorate each to represent the two concession stands described in the play. At the top of one stand place a sign that reads "Ice Cream 5¢ and 10¢," and on the other place a sign that reads "Zalabia 5¢." When the play opens, keep some distance between the two stands. Hang a sign behind them that reads "St. Louis World's Fair."

Costumes for the characters will add ambience to the play. Consider the period (1904) and have the students dress accordingly. Even bowler hats and handlebar mustaches for boys and full, long skirts and straw hats for girls will help to set the stage.

## History of the Ice Cream Cone

The first ice cream cone was made in 1896 by an Italian immigrant named Italo Marchiony. He created the cone in New York City and got a patent for it in 1903. In 1904, at the St. Louis World's Fair, an ice cream vendor was selling dishes of ice cream for five and ten cents. The ice cream sold so well that the vendor ran out of dishes. The vendor next door offered one of his wafer-thin waffle pastries to solve the problem. The Middle Eastern pastry, called zalabia, was made by the Syrian chef Ernest A. Hamwi. He rolled one of his zalabia into the shape of a cone, and it cooled into a crisp ice cream cone within moments. The "cornucopias," as they were called, were an immediate success.

Shortly after the fair, enterprising business people all around St. Louis began designing special equipment to make the cones cheaply and efficiently. Stephen Sullivan, a Missouri businessman, became the first known independent operator in the new business of ice cream cone production. In 1906 he served the cones (still called cornucopias) at the Modern Woodsmen of America Frisco Log Rolling in Sullivan, Missouri. At the same time, the Syrian zalabia maker, Ernest Hamwi, developed the Cornucopia Waffle Company. In 1910, he founded the Missouri Cone Company, which later became known as the Western Cone Company. Ice cream cones were well on their way to mass popularity.

In 1924 the production of ice cream cones had reached a record-breaking 254 million. Today, modern machinery can produce cones at 150,000 every day. They have become one of the biggest-selling American treats.

# How the Ice Cream Cone Came to Be *(cont.)*

## Characters:

Mary Peterson (*a fictional name for a real person*)
Ernest Hamwi
Customer 1
Customer 2

Customer 3
Customer 4
additional customers (*walking around the fair*)

**Setting:** St. Louis World's Fair, 1904

| **Scene 1:** | *The two vendors are setting up their concession booths next to one another.* |

**Mary:** (*walking over to Ernest and holding out her hand*): Hello there. My name is Mary Peterson. I am going to sell ice cream in this stand.

**Ernest:** (*shaking Mary's hand*) I am pleased to meet you. My name is Ernest Hamwi. I am going to sell a food called zalabia. It is from Syria, where I was born.

**Mary:** I've never heard of zalabia. What is it?

**Ernest:** It is something like American waffles. Here, try one. (He hands her a zalabia.)

**Mary:** (*tasting it*) That's wonderful! Thank you. Would you like to try some of my ice cream? I have vanilla and strawberry.

**Ernest:** Yes, I'd like a taste of the strawberry, please.

(*Mary scoops it into a dish and hands it to Ernest. He tastes it.*)

**Ernest:** That's very good. Thank you.

(*Mary and Ernest finish their treats.*)

**Mary:** Well, I had better finish setting up my stand. They say there will be quite a crowd here today.

**Ernest:** I heard the same. Well, good luck!

# How the Ice Cream Cone Came to Be *(cont.)*

| | |
|---|---|
| **Scene 2:** | The scene opens on Ernest and Mary's concession stands later in the day. Several customers walk by. |

**Mary:** (*calling out to the customers*) Ice cream! Ice cream! Get your ice-cold ice cream! Five cents for a single scoop! Ten cents for a double scoop! Get your ice cream here!

**Ernest:** (*calling out to the customers*) Zalabia! Zalabia! Fresh off the grill! A delicious waffle treat from Syria! Get your zalabia here!

**Customer 1:** (*going to the ice cream stand*) Mmm! I'll try some of that. Give me a single scoop of vanilla, please.

**Customer 2:** (*also going to the ice cream stand*) Ice cream! Sounds great! May I have a double vanilla, please?

**Customer 3:** (*with a quizzical look*) Zalabia? What's zalabia? (*Goes to the ice cream stand.*) I'll have a single strawberry, please.

**Customer 4:** (*going to the zalabia stand*) I'll try that. It sounds interesting.

(*All customers taste their treats.*)

**Customer 4:** (*to another customer*) Hmm. This is good, but it seems to be missing something.

**Customers 1, 2, and 3:** Mmm, delicious.

(*Several additional customers mill about the ice cream stand. A few go to the zalabia stand.*)

**Mary:** (*calling to Ernest when the crowd disperses*) How's business?

**Ernest:** Good enough, but I would like to think of a way to make it better.

**Mary:** Really? My ice cream is selling like hot cakes. (*Laughs at her joke.*) But it is going much faster than I thought it would. It's great business, but I am just about ready to run out of dishes. I don't know what I'll do then.

**Ernest:** (*thoughtfully*) Oh, really? I wonder what can be done about that?

**Mary:** If you think of something, let me know. I can't leave now to buy more dishes. Any idea you have would be helpful.

**Ernest:** I'll think about it and let you know what I come up with.

**Mary:** Thanks!

# How the Ice Cream Cone Came To Be *(cont.)*

| Scene 3: | Back at the stands later in the same day. |
|---|---|

**Ernest:** (*excitedly going to Mary's stand, holding a rolled zalabia*) Mary, I have it!

**Mary:** Have what, Ernest?

**Ernest:** A way to solve your problem—and mine!

**Mary:** Great! What is it?

**Ernest:** My zalabia! See, if I roll it into a cone shape as soon as it comes off the grill, it cools in a few moments, and voila! We have a cornucopia. Get the idea? Try putting a scoop or two of your ice cream inside.

**Mary:** (*catching his excitement*) Okay, let's see how it works. (*She tries it.*) Perfect! But it still has to pass the final test. Let's taste it. Roll another zalabia, please.

*(Ernest rolls another cone, and Mary fills it with ice cream. They hold up their cones and use them to toast like champagne glasses, and then they try their new treat. They smile with pleasure.)*

**Mary:** Ernest, my ice cream is even better this way. This is a lucky day for me.

**Ernest:** Me, too! The customers are going to love this.

**Mary:** I think a partnership is called for. What do you say?

**Ernest:** I agree: "The Great Cornucopia Cone Concession."

**Mary:** Another good idea! Let's get rolling. (*She laughs at her joke.*)

*(Mary and Ernest shake hands. Then they push their two stands together and put up a new sign that reads "The Great Cornucopia Cone Concession." The customers take notice.)*

**Mary:** (*calling out to the customers*) Ice cream in a cornucopia! All new! You'll taste it here for the first time at the St. Louis World's Fair! Ten cents for a single scoop! Fifteen cents for a double! Try our delicious ice cream in a cornucopia!

**Ernest:** (*to the audience*) Zalabia and ice cream . . . I think this is the start of a delicious friendship.

# Freezing Ice Cream

Do the following experiment as a class or in small groups to observe what happens as ice cream freezes.

## Materials:

- 2 cups (480 mL) chilled cream
- ½ teaspoon (2.5 mL) vanilla
- one 5 oz. (150 mL) paper cup
- finely crushed ice (or snow, if available)
- 2 craft sticks
- ½ cup (120 mL) white sugar
- plastic jug or similar container
- one 8–10 oz. (240–300 mL) Styrofoam cup
- 4 tablespoons (60 mL) table salt
- large jug or pitcher

## Directions:

1. Mix the cream, sugar, and vanilla together in the jug.

2. Pour some of the cream mixture into the paper cup, filling it half to three-quarters full. Keep it cold.

3. Fill the Styrofoam cup about one-third full with ice (snow).

4. Add about 3–4 tablespoons (45–60 mL) salt to the ice.

5. Mark one stick "ice." Use it to stir the salt into the ice.

6. Make a hole in the ice big enough to fit the paper cup so that the ice surrounds, but does not flow into, the cream mixture.

7. Mark the other stick "cream." Stir the ice cream mixture slowly, scraping the newly formed crystals from the bottom and sides of the cup and stopping from time to time to let the ice cream solidify. You may have to stir for about 30 minutes until the ice cream is ready to eat—icy and slightly soft.

# Ice Cream Facts

As you study ice cream, collect science facts about its composition. Students can also be assigned to find ice cream science facts for homework. Then make fact books according to the following directions.

## Materials:

- 6" x 18" (15 cm x 45 cm) construction paper
- 6" x 18" (15 cm x 45 cm) white paper
- glue sticks
- pencils
- scissors
- pattern

## Directions:

1. Glue a sheet of white paper to a sheet of construction paper.
2. Fold the left and right sides of the paper inward, in thirds, so that the folded paper makes a square.
3. Trace the scoop pattern onto the top fold. Cut it out through all three folds.
4. Write an ice cream fact on each page of the three-fold book. Write "Ice Cream Facts" on the cover.

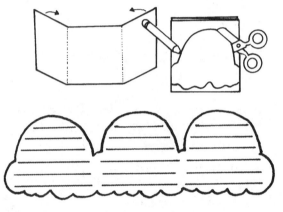

# Taste Buds

Taste buds cover your tongue. The interesting thing about a taste bud is its location in the mouth determines how something will taste when that item touches the taste bud. Have students try this experiment.

**Materials:**

- sugar
- lemon juice
- salt
- tonic water
- patterns (page 60)
- scissors
- crayons
- glue

**Directions:**

1. Ask the students to sprinkle a little sugar on their tongues, paying attention to where the sugar is when they taste it. This is where their taste buds for sweet foods are located.

2. Do the same with the remaining materials, one at a time. Lemon juice will find their sour buds, salt will find their salt buds, and the tonic water will find their bitter buds.

3. Have the students color the tongue pattern according to the directions on the next page.

4. Have the students cut the mouth on the face pattern and insert the tongue through the mouth. Glue it in place as shown.

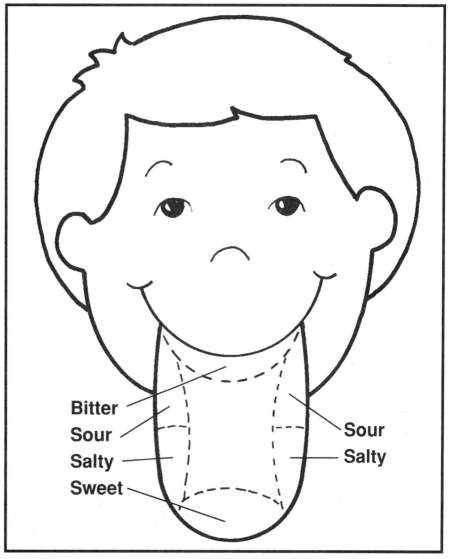

**Bitter**
**Sour**
**Salty**
**Sweet**
**Sour**
**Salty**

# Taste Buds *(cont.)*

**Student Directions:** Color the **sweet** place on the tongue **green.** Color the **sour** places on the tongue **yellow.** Color the **bitter** place on the tongue **red.** Color the **salty** place on your tongue **blue.**

glue tab

# Baking Ice Cream

How can you bake ice cream without melting it?  Try this to find out.

**Materials:**

- 1 pint (600 mL) ice cream
- 3 egg whites
- 1/8 cup (25 g) sugar
- 6 hard cookies
- tray
- ice cream scoop
- cookie sheet
- freezer
- oven
- oven mitt
- spatula

**Directions:**

1. Lay the cookies 2–3 inches (5–8 cm) apart on a tray.

2. Place one scoop of ice cream on each cookie.

3. Put the tray in the freezer until the ice cream is very firm.  (Do this the first thing in the morning so that it will be ready in the afternoon.)

4. When the ice cream is firm, preheat your oven to 450°F (230°C).

5. Prepare meringue by beating the egg whites until they peak.  Gradually add the sugar while continuing to beat the egg whites.

6. Remove the ice cream cookies from the freezer.  Place them on an ungreased cookie sheet.  (If you freeze the cookie sheet, it may warp in the oven.)

7. Cover each ice cream cookie with a thick layer of meringue.  Be sure to cover the ice cream and cookie completely, forming a seal with the cookie sheet.

8. Bake the ice cream cookie in the oven for 2 to 3 minutes, just until the meringue turns light brown.  Remove immediately.

9. Peek inside.  The ice cream has not melted! Ask the students if they have any guesses as to why this is.

**The Trick:** The meringue serves as insulation, protecting the ice cream from the heat.  Many tiny air bubbles form when the egg is beaten.  These bubbles slow down the passage of heat through the meringue.  Since the ice cream is baked for so short a time, the heat does not have enough time to pass through the meringue and melt the ice cream.

# Here's the Scoop

## Stuffed and Stitched Cones

**Materials:**

- brown wrapping paper or bags
- pencils
- scissors
- markers or crayons
- paints and brushes
- yardstick (meterstick)
- newspaper
- hole punch
- yarn

**Directions:**

1. Draw a large ice cream cone (with a scoop of ice cream) on the paper or flattened bag, approximately 18" x 24" (45 cm x 60 cm). Keep the shape simple and a little fatter than it would normally be. Cut it out.
2. Trace to make a second copy of the shape. Cut it out.
3. Paint the ice cream any "flavor." Be sure to paint it on both patterns.
4. Use a dark brown marker or crayon and a yardstick (meterstick) to "waffle" the cone on both patterns.
5. Place the patterns back to back. Punch holes through both patterns about 1" (2.5 cm) apart.
6. Beginning at the top, stitch through the holes with yarn, leaving a length of yarn where you begin and leaving an opening at the top.
7. Stuff the patterns loosely with wadded newspaper.
8. Finish stitching the patterns together and tie off the yarn. Use the leftover length of yarn left out as a hanger. Suspend the cone from the ceiling or lights.

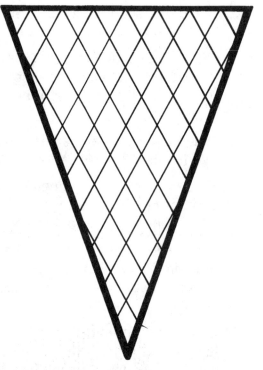

## Ice Cream Collages

**Materials:**

- old newspapers
- brown wrapping paper or bags
- pencils
- scissors
- markers or crayons
- yardstick (meterstick)
- glue
- pencil

**Directions:**

1. Follow steps 1 and 4 above, making only one pattern per student or student group.
2. Have each student or group choose an ice cream flavor. They can then cut or tear out pictures from magazines the color of that flavor.
3. Glue the pictures to the ice cream on the cone.
4. Cut out the cones and hang them around the room.

# Ice Cream Truck

In many towns and cities, the ice cream truck carries delicious ice cream novelties throughout the neighborhoods. An ice cream novelty is a manufactured ice cream or other frozen treat sold on an ice cream truck. Make your own ice cream truck using the following materials and directions.

**Materials:**

- wheel and truck patterns
- fine point markers or pens
- crayons

- scissors
- brass fasteners

**Directions:**

1. Brainstorm for a list of ice cream novelties.

2. Use a marker or pen to make a sign on the truck pattern, listing these ice cream novelties.

3. Color the rest of the truck, wheels, and driver.

4. Cut out the truck and wheels.

5. Attach the wheels to the truck at the Xs. Use the brass fasteners.

6. Display your trucks around the room.

**Ice Cream Sold Here**
- Eskimo Pies
- Scooter Pies
- Push-Ups
- Drumsticks
- Sidewalk Sundaes
- Snowcones
- Popsicles
- Ice Cream Sandwiches

**Alternative:** If you have a class ice cream party for parents, use the truck patterns as menus for the items being served.

# Ice Cream Truck *(cont.)*

**truck pattern**

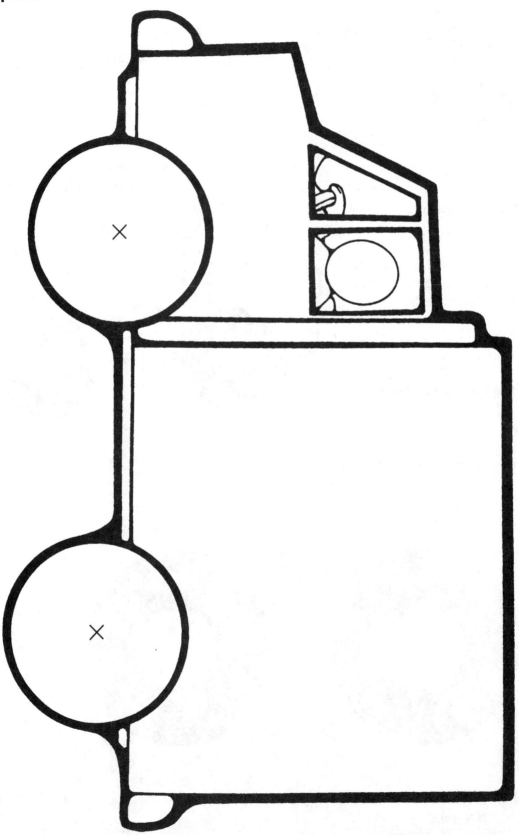

64

# Ice Cream Songs

Sing the following songs written to familiar tunes.  Then have the class write others in the same way?

## Take Me Out for Some Ice Cream

*(sung to the tune of "Take Me Out to the Ball Game")*

Take me out for some ice cream,

Take me out to the store.

Buy me a triple scoop jumbo cone.

I won't share; I will eat it alone!

So just scoop, scoop, scoop up the ice cream —

Give me three kinds I adore!

For it's one, two, three scoops to go

At the ice cream store!

## Hot Fudge, Cherries, Toffee Crunch

*(sung to the tune of "Twinkle, Twinkle, Little Star")*

Hot fudge, cherries, toffee crunch,

Peanuts, whipped cream, lots to munch.

At the top of my ice cream,

So delicious, it's a dream!

Hot fudge, cherries, toffee crunch,

How I love to munch and munch!

## Dip Deep the Silver Scoop

*(sung to the tune of "Swing Low, Sweet Chariot")*

Dip deep the silver scoop
Into the chocolate ice cream.
Dip deep the silver scoop
Into the chocolate ice cream.

I looked o'er the counter, and what did I see
Right by the chocolate ice cream?
Lots of hot fudge, caramel, and strawberry
To add to my chocolate ice cream.

Dip deep the silver scoop
And have some delicious ice cream.
Try a bite, or two, or three
Of this delicious ice cream.

## The Ice Cream in the Bowl

*(sung to the tune of "The Farmer in the Dell")*

The ice cream in the bowl,
The ice cream in the bowl,
Hi-ho the dairy-o,
The ice cream in the bowl.

The ice cream takes a banana.
The ice cream takes a banana.
Hi-ho the dairy-o,
The ice cream takes a banana.

The banana takes some fudge (etc.).
The fudge takes some sprinkles (etc.).
The sprinkles take some nuts (etc.).
The nuts take some whipped cream (etc.).
The whipped cream takes a cherry (etc.).
The cherry takes a child (etc.).
The child eats the sundae (etc.).

# Ice Cream Relay

The entire class can participate in an exciting, theme-based relay.  Just follow these directions.

**Materials:**
- ice cream cones
- foam balls that fit atop the cones (available from craft stores)
- pylons (or other markers)

**Directions:**
1. Divide the students into teams of at least four members each.  Give each team one cone and one foam ball.  The foam balls will serve as scoops of ice cream.
2. Place as many pylons as you have teams in a line about 2–3 feet (1 meter) apart.  Place another row of pylons at an equal distance across from the first.
3. Divide each team in half.  Half of each team will stand in line behind a pylon on one side and the other half behind the pylon straight across.  The first person in line on one side will hold a cone and a scoop.
4. At your command, the relay will begin.  Players with the cone will run across to the rest of their team on the other side, holding their ice cream cone by the cone only.  (They cannot touch the scoop.)  Once they arrive at the other end, they will hand off their cones to the first players in line.  Then they move to the back of the lines.
5. The player who now has the cone runs across as before and hands off to the first player in line at the opposite side.
6. Play continues until all members of one team have run with the cone and the last runner passes the pylon on the opposite side.
7. If desired, give the certificate below to the members of the winning team.

## Cone-gratulations

_____!

name

You are an Ice Cream Relay champ!

_____    _____

teacher                      date

# Ice Cream in a Bag

On this and the following page are two methods for making ice cream. This recipe can be done in groups or pairs. It is an excellent choice for learning centers.

**Materials and Ingredients:**

- 1 large resealable plastic bag
- 1 small resealable plastic bag
- ice cubes
- rock salt

- 1 cup (250 mL) whipping cream
- ¼ cup (60 mL) sugar
- ¼ teaspoon (1.25 mL) vanilla

**Directions:**

1. In a mixing bowl, combine whipping cream, sugar, and vanilla. Place this mixture in the small bag and seal well.

2. Combine the ice and rock salt in the large bag, filling the bag about one-third full with ice. Adjustments for ice and salt may be needed during the experiment.

3. Put the small plastic bag inside the large one. Seal the large bag well and shake it.

4. In a short while, the contents of the smaller bag should thicken to the consistency of soft ice cream or frozen yogurt. Add more ice or salt to the large bag and drain water from it, as needed. Shake until the ice cream reaches a desired thickness.

**Extension:**

Use this activity as a science experiment. Before beginning, make predictions as to what will happen and how long it will take. Make observations throughout the experiment. Afterwards, have students write a paragraph about what happened and why the students think it happened.

# Coffee Can Ice Cream

**Materials and Ingredients:**

- 3 lb. (1.35 kg) coffee can and lid
- 1 lb. (.45 kg) coffee can and lid
- masking tape
- wire whisk
- 1 cup (250 mL) whipping cream
- ½ cup (125 mL) sugar

- 1 cup (250 mL) milk
- 1 teaspoon (5 mL) vanilla
- small paper cups and spoons
- crushed ice
- rock salt

**Directions:**

| | | |
|---|---|---|
| 1. Mix the whipping cream, sugar, milk, and vanilla in the small coffee can.<br> | 2. Put on the lid tightly and tape it to prevent leakage.<br> | 3. Put a thin layer of ice and rock salt in the large coffee can.<br> |
| 4. Place the smaller coffee can inside the larger one and fill up all the excess space with ice and about 1 cup (250 mL) rock salt.<br> | 5. Put on the lid as before.<br> | 6. Find an area on the floor where a small group of students can sit about 5 feet (2 meters) apart from one another. Have the students roll the coffee can back and forth for about 15 minutes, checking after 10 minutes to see if the mixture in the smaller can is becoming ice cream. When ready, serve and enjoy. This recipe yields about 3 cups (750 mL). |

**Extension:**

After making the ice cream on this page or the previous one, have the students taste it and then taste some store-bought ice cream. Individually or in small groups, ask them to complete a Venn diagram comparison of the two ice creams.

# Culminating Activities

## Ice Cream Social

An ice cream social would be an enjoyable way to end the unit and one that would not take a great deal of planning. Have the students make invitations to send to their parents, inviting them in for your social. Bring in (or have donated) a variety of ice creams and ask visiting parents each to bring in a topping of some kind. For students who are allergic to milk, or those who are lactose intolerant, provide some soy or rice milk ice cream. Provide bowls and spoons and let the students and parents make their own treats. Display the work done throughout the unit and provide entertainment, if desired. The play on pages 53–56 would be fitting.

## Ice Cream Truck

This culminating activity will take some preparatory work, but it will be well worth the effort. Before beginning, get approval from the proper school authorities to sell ice cream novelties. Get approval from not only the school principal and/or activities coordinator, but the cafeteria supervisor as well. In many schools, whatever food items are sold must either go directly through the cafeteria or, at least, not be in direct competition with it.

**The Truck:** Make it out of two large appliance boxes (refrigerator size). Cut out one side panel from each and affix the boxes together at their openings so that the two horizontal boxes will become one. Use the panels you removed as wall reinforcement on the inside walls. Cut a door on one side for the vendor(s) to enter and exit and cut out a window from which to sell. (Cut the window along two sides and the bottom only so that you can fold it up like an awning. Attach it up with string.) Paint the truck inside and out to look like an ice cream truck. You can paint the front windshield or actually cut it out.

**The Menu:** For example, you might sell Eskimo Pies, Ice Cream Sandwiches, and Popsicles. Price the items. Ask your school cafeteria about the best vendors from whom you might purchase the novelties at a low cost. Once you know how much they will cost, plan your selling prices, determining what your per item profit will be (and to whom or for what your profits will go). Make a menu, including prices, to be placed on the side of your truck.

**Freezing:** If possible, locate your truck near the cafeteria to make use of its refrigeration. If not, pool parents for the possibility of a freezer loan. At the very least, pack tubs on ice and plan on a relatively short selling time.

**Hats:** Each vendor should wear a hat. Copy and cut out three hat patterns (page 70) for each student. For each child, place the pattern strips end to end and glue, tape, or staple them together to fit around the child's head. Students can color the stripes at the top of the hats in alternating white and red, or any colors you desire, and leave the bottom portion white.

**Advertisement:** Make advertisements that include where and when the truck will be open for service. Post the advertisements around school, and if the truck will serve during an after-school event, send home advertisements to the parents.

## Ice Cream Parlor

Follow directions for the ice cream truck, altering the boxes to look like the facade of an ice cream parlor. Plan a variety of ice cream specialties and serve them to parents during a class party or as a fundraiser during any desired school event.

# Culminating Activities *(cont.)*

**Hat Pattern**

hat bottom

hat top

# Bookmarks and Incentives

Build an ice cream cone, scoop by scoop, for each book read or each task completed. Let students see how many scoops their cones can grow! Cones can also be used for student jobs. Write the jobs on the cones and student names on the scoops. Switch the scoops as needed when it is time to change jobs.

**Reading is a treat.**

I scream You scream We all scream For reading!

# Sweet Ideas

## Bulletin Board Ideas

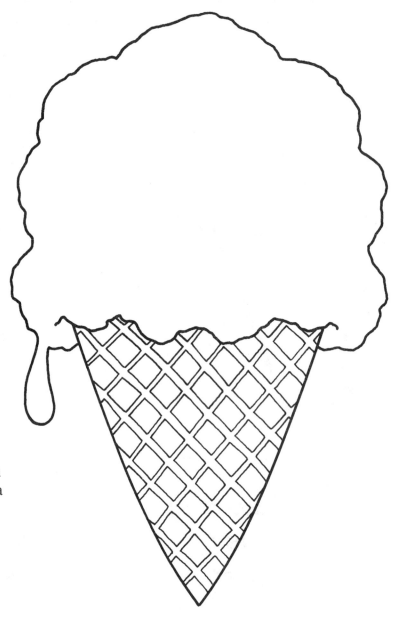

1. Using the ice cream cone pattern on this page, make (or have students make) a cone for every student in the class. Write a student's name on each cone. Cover a bulletin board with white paper. Make an awning, that lies flat, out of white and red construction paper or cut and fold tagboard to make an awning that protrudes. Have the class choose a name for their classroom "ice cream parlor." Under the awning, write "Welcome to (name) Ice Cream Parlor." Under the greeting, place the name cones in a row.

2. Reproduce and cut out the scoop and cone patterns on pages 73 and 74. Adjust pattern sizes according to your needs.

   (You may wish to reproduce the scoops on a variety of paper colors to represent different flavors of ice cream.) Write each student's name on a cone. Place the cones on a large bulletin board or display them around the room. Use the cone as a means of rewarding a student for his or her achievement or skill mastery by writing the appropriate reward information on a scoop. Add a scoop for each new achievement.

## Chalkboard Magnets

Many chalkboards have a metal backing so magnets can be used to hold pictures, charts, lists, and so forth. To make magnets, you can copy the small magnet patterns on page 74, color them, cut them out, and attach a magnetic strip to the back of each with glue. (The strips can be purchased at a craft store.) You can also purchase small white, brown, and pink pompons and brown felt at a craft store. Glue one, two, or three pompons to the top of a cone-shaped piece of felt and affix a magnetic strip to the back. You have a fluffy ice cream cone!

# Sweet Ideas *(cont.)*

See page 72 for instructions.

## Ice Cream

# Sweet Ideas *(cont.)*

See page 72 for instructions.

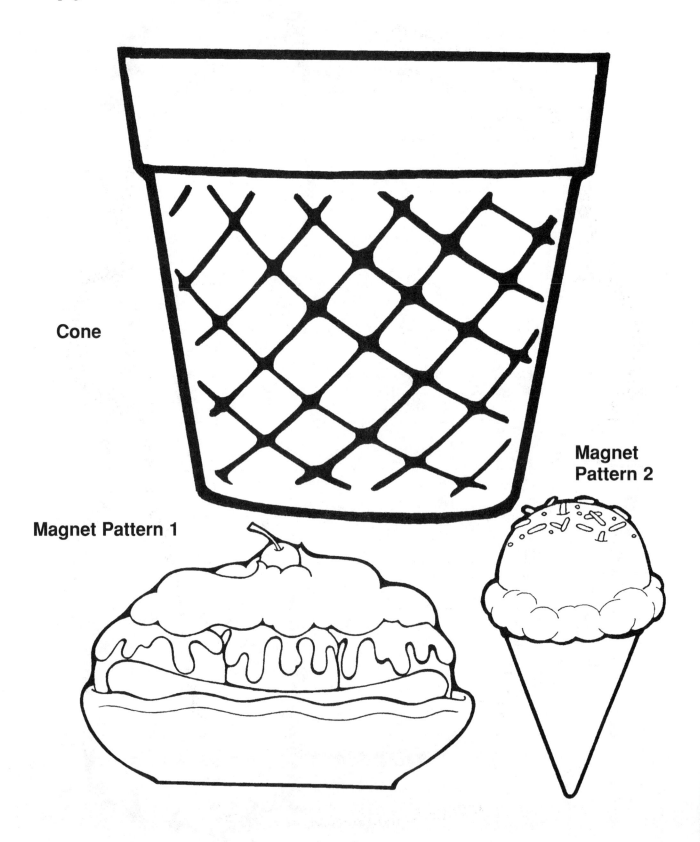

**Cone**

**Magnet Pattern 2**

**Magnet Pattern 1**

74

# Ice Cream Stationery

# Unit Award

This certificate is presented to

_____
name

on the _____ day of _____
              day              month

_____
year

for excellent work on our
Ice Cream Unit.

It is a treat having you in class!

_____
teacher

# Letter to Parents

**Teacher Note:** Duplicate the letter below, filling in the information that pertains to your needs.

Dear Parents,

We will be studying a unit on ice cream. Ice cream is an excellent theme selection since it offers a variety of ways to learn important concepts in all areas of the curriculum. We are going to be very busy doing many things, and in order to facilitate our learning possible, we would like to ask for your help. We will need the following supplies to complete our unit:

_____

_____

_____

_____

_____

_____

_____

If you can donate any of these supplies, please send them with your child by

_____ .

------------------------------------------------

We can use help in the classroom during the following times:

_____

Please circle any times that you can come. Return the bottom portion of this letter with your child by

_____

Thanks! You are the cherry on our sundaes!

_____
signature

_____ _____
parent name                              daytime phone

# Bibliography

Berger, Melvin. *Make Mine Ice Cream.* Newbridge, 1993.

Busenberg, Bonnie. *Vanilla, Chocolate & Strawberry.* Lerner Publishing, 1994.

Cobb, Vicki. *The Scoop on Ice Cream.* Little, Brown, and Company, 1985.

Damerow, Gail. *Ice Cream: The Whole Scoop.* Glenbridge Publishing, 1991.

Dickson, Paul. *The Great American Ice Cream Book.* Atheneum, 1976.

Duecker, Joyce S. *The Old-Fashioned Homemade Ice Cream Cookbook.* Bobbs-Merrill, 1974.

Greenberg, Keith E. *Ben & Jerry: Ice Cream for Everyone.* Blackbirch, 1994.

Hoffman, Mable. *Ice Cream.* H.P. Books, 1981.

Hurwitz, Joanna. *Aldo Ice Cream.* Puffin, 1981.

Jackson-Dilling, Gayle. *Thematic Unit: Ice Cream.* Teacher Created Materials, 1996.

Jaspersohn, William. *Ice Cream.* Macmillan, 1988.

Keller, Stella. *Ice Cream.* Raintree Steck-Vaughn, 1989.

Klein, Matthew. *The Joy of Ice Cream.* Barron's, 1985.

Krensky, Stephen. *Scoop After Scoop: A History of Ice Cream.* Atheneum, 1986.

Kroll, Steven. *The Hokey-Pokey Man.* Holiday House, 1989.

Lager, Fred. *Ben & Jerry's: The Inside Scoop.* Crown, 1994.

Lexau, J. *Striped Ice Cream.* Lippincott, 1968.

Liddell, Caroline. *Frozen Desserts.* St. Martin's Griffin, 1996.

Lobel, Arnold. "Ice Cream" in *Frog and Toad All Year.* HarperCollins, 1976.

*Luncheonette: Ice Cream, Beverage, and Sandwich Recipes from the Golden Age of the Soda Fountain.* Crown, 1989.

Mitgutsch, Ali. *From Milk to Ice Cream.* Carolrhoda Books, 1979.

Neimark, Jill. *Ice Cream!* Hastings House, 1986.

Prelutsky, Jack. "Bleezer's Ice Cream" in *The New Kid on the Block.* Greenwillow Books, 1984.

Prelutsky, Jack. "Herbert Glerbett" in *The Random House Book of Poetry for Children.* Random House, 1983.

Rey, Margret and Alan J, Shalleck. *Curious George Goes to an Ice Cream Shop.* Houghton Mifflin, 1979.

Silverstein, Shel. "Eighteen Flavors" in *Where the Sidewalk Ends.* Harper and Row, 1974.

Siracusa, Catherine. *The Banana Split from Outer Space.* Hyperion, 1995.

Spitler, Sue. *Wild About Ice Cream.* Barron's, 1985.

Tice, Patricia. *Ice Cream for All.* Strong Music, 1990.

Walden, Hilary. *Ice Cream: Over 400 Variations, from Simple Scoops to Spectacular Desserts.* Simon and Schuster, 1985.

Warner, Gertrude Chandler. *The Chocolate Sundae Mystery.* Albert Whitman & Company, 1995.

For more information about ice cream, write to

National Dairy Council
6300 North River Road
Rosemont, IL 60018

# Answer Key

**Page 8**

The man with the yellow hat takes George to an ice cream shop.

The shop owner says he has just opened the place.

The man with the yellow hat chooses his flavor cone.

Mr. Herb answers a phone call.

George scoops ice cream into Mr. Herb's special order.

Mr. Herb is angry with George.

George builds a banana split at the front counter.

A crowd watches George.

Many people come into Mr. Herb's shop.

Mr. Herb thanks George.

**Page 12**

5 + 4 = 9
5 + 2 = 7
2 + 6 = 8
13 − 6 = 7
15 − 7 = 8
8 + 0 = 8
11 − 2 = 9
6 + 1 = 7
1 + 7 = 8
2 + 7 = 9
0 + 9 = 9
15 − 6 = 9
12 − 4 = 8
12 − 3 = 9
11 − 4 = 7
5 + 3 = 8
10 − 3 = 7
3 + 6 = 9
3 + 4 = 7
15 − 8 = 7

**Page 16**

Frog and Toad sit by the pond on a hot, summer day.

Frog wants some ice cream.

Toad decides to get ice cream for Frog and himself.

Toad buys two chocolate cones.

The hot sun begins to melt the cones.

The cones drip all over Toad, covering him with ice cream.

A frightened mouse runs past Frog.

A squirrel tells Frog that a creature is coming.

Toad falls in the pond.

Frog and Toad go together to buy chocolate cones.

**Page 26**

Mix and Blend
Pasteurize
Homogenize
Cool
Store
Add Coloring and Flavoring
Whip and Freeze
Add Fruits, Nuts, and Candies
Package
Freeze Until Hard

**Page 37**

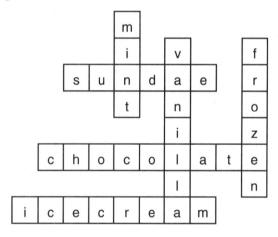

**Page 38**

1. mint
2. vanilla
3. neapolitan
4. caramel swirl
5. vanilla fudge
6. chocolate
7. mocha
8. chocolate chip
9. strawberry
10. bubblegum
11. lemon
12. rocky road
13. lime
14. butter pecan
15. fudge ripple

# Answer Key *(cont.)*

**Page 42**

20 - 8 = 12 (red)
17 - 0 = 17 (brown)
19 - 3 = 16 (pink)
17 - 7 = 10 (yellow)
15 - 1 = 14 (orange)
19 - 6 = 13 (blue)
14 - 3 = 11 (purple)
20 - 5 = 15 (green)

**Page 43**

1. 4
2. 2
3. 2
4. 4
5. 16
6. 8

**Page 44**

1. 10
2. 10
3. 10
4. 100
5. 1,000

**Page 46**

1. $8.00
2. $4.75
3. $5.75
4. $12.25

**Page 47**

1. $10 + 6 = 16$
2. $17 - 8 = 9$
3. $13 + 4 = 17$
4. $9 + 10 = 19$
5. $8 - 7 = 1$
6. $15 + 4 = 19$
7. $18 - 11 = 7$
8. $21 - 16 = 5$
9. $20 + 9 = 29$
10. $14 - 7 = 7$
11. $23 - 13 = 10$
12. $14 + 11 = 25$
13. $14 - 6 = 8$
14. $6 + 13 = 19$
15. $12 + 12 = 24$
16. $18 - 6 = 12$

**Page 52**

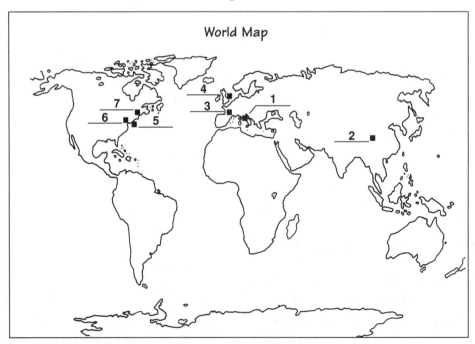

World Map